Jobs People Do

Veterinarians

by Mary Meinking

PEBBLE
a capstone imprint

Pebble Explore is published by Pebble, an imprint of Capstone.
1710 Roe Crest Drive
North Mankato, Minnesota 56003
www.capstonepub.com

Library of Congress Cataloging-in-Publication Data is available on the Library of Congress website.
ISBN: 978-1-9771-1381-8 (hardcover)
ISBN: 978-1-9771-1816-5 (paperback)
ISBN: 978-1-9771-1389-4 (eBook PDF)

Summary: Veterinarians care for all kinds of animals. Readers will find out the tools vets use, the different types of veterinarians, and how people get this caring and exciting job.

Image Credits
iStockphoto: andresr, 25, fotografixx, 9, kali9, 14; Newscom: Smithsonian Institute/Jessie Cohen, 18; Science Source: William D. Bachman, 21; Shutterstock: ARTFULLY PHOTOGRAPHER, 22, Daisy Daisy, 17, JPC-PROD, 1, Kzenon, 19, Lucky Business, 15, New Africa, 8, nimon, Cover, PRESSLAB, 23, Serhii Bobyk, 26, Susan Schmitz, 11, Syda Productions, 7, Tyler Olson, 5, XiXinXing, 13; Wikimedia/CDC, 28

Editorial Credits
Editor: Gena Chester; Designer: Kyle Grenz; Media Researcher: Jo Miller; Production Specialist: Kathy McColley

All internet sites appearing in back matter were available and accurate when this book was sent to press.

Printed and bound in the USA.
PA99

Table of Contents

Words in **bold** are in the glossary.

What Is a Veterinarian?

A small dog runs into the waiting room. Its owner holds on to its leash. A cat sitting on its owner's lap starts hissing. The veterinarian, or vet, comes into the room.

Vets are animal doctors. They take care of animals of all sizes. When animals get sick, they can't tell us what is wrong. Vets make sure animals get better.

Pets and farm animals need vets. Zoo animals need vets too. Vets keep animals healthy.

Most vets grow up loving animals. Vets need to be good with animals and people. They need to explain the animal's problems to people.

Vets are good at fixing problems. They find out why an animal is sick. Vets love working with animals. Every day is something new.

What Veterinarians Do

Vets care for animals. Regular vet visits are important. Vets make sure animals eat the right foods. They also want animals to get enough **exercise**.

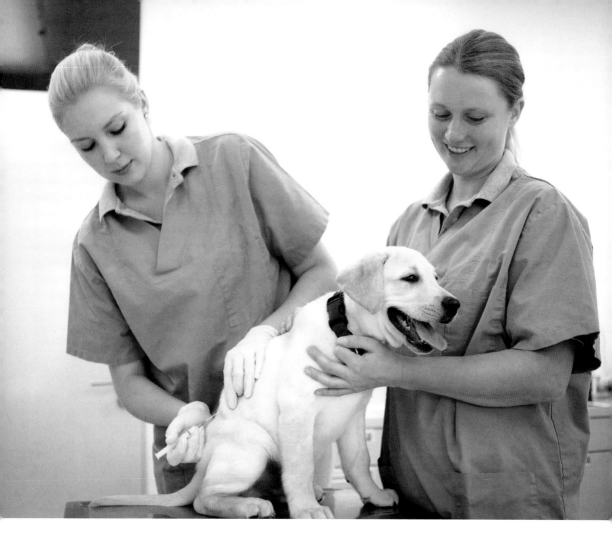

Some animals need help having babies. Vets help animals give birth. They give shots to the baby animals. Shots keep animals healthy. Most animals get shots every few years.

People know their pets well. If their pets are sick, they take the pets to a vet. Some vets work long hours to help sick animals. They check an animal for what could be wrong. Vets might give **medicine** to animals. Medicine helps animals feel better.

Sometimes animals get hurt. Vets can help animals get better. They may fix broken bones or close cuts. An animal might need **surgery**. A vet can do many different kinds of surgery.

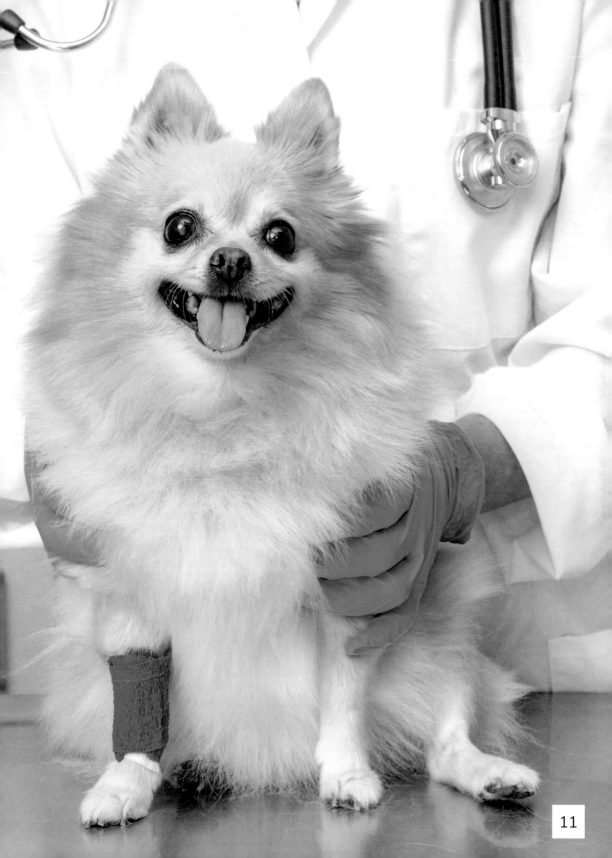

11

How Veterinarians Help

Many people love their pets. They get upset when their pets aren't well. Vets gently explain what is wrong with their pets. Vets do their best to help people stay calm.

Animals might act out when they are sick. They can bite, claw, or kick. A vet tries to keep animals calm. When an animal is calm, then the vet can check an animal's body.

Many vets help at animal **shelters**.
They make sure animals are healthy
before going to new homes.

A vet uses a tool to put a chip under the cat's skin.

Lost pets end up in shelters. A vet can help keep pets from getting lost. They can place a tiny chip under an animal's skin. If the pet is lost, people can read the chip to find its owner.

Where Veterinarians Work

Most vets work at small animal hospitals. They help pets such as dogs, cats, birds, or hamsters.

Other vets work outside with large animals. They help animals such as cows, horses, or sheep. Vets drive to see these animals.

Some vets only take care of horses. These vets care for horses at farms or ranches.

Vets also work in zoos and **aquariums**. They know how to care for all kinds of animals. Elephants, monkeys, tigers, and fish all need vets.

Other vets work for big companies.
They create new foods, tools, or
medicines for animals.

Some vets work at colleges. They
teach animal care to people who want
to be vets someday.

Veterinarians' Clothes and Tools

In offices, vets wear long white coats over their clothes. Some wear **scrubs**. During surgery, they wear shoe covers, masks, gloves, and caps.

Vets who work outdoors can get dirty. They wear tall rubber boots. Some also wear one-piece coveralls. These keep their clothes clean.

coveralls

boots

21

A vet's tools look like a doctor's tools. A vet uses a **stethoscope**. This tool listens to an animal's heart and lungs. A vet also has tools to look in an animal's ears, eyes, and throat.

stethoscope

A vet looks at an X-ray to check for broken bones.

Vets have different tools for different types of animals. They may use scissors or knives in surgery.

Vets also use an **X-ray** machine. This takes pictures of bones. It helps a vet find broken bones.

How to Become a Veterinarian

Anyone can become a vet. They need to like animals and care about them.

People can work with animals before becoming a vet. They can help at animal hospitals, shelters, or farms. They can clean cages or feed animals. Or they might help wash or walk animals.

It takes eight years of schooling to become a vet. First, people need four years of college. They might study science. Then they apply for vet school. There they study animal medicine for four more years. People also work with animals in vet school.

After school, they must pass tests. Before new vets can work on their own, they must work with older vets.

Some vets take more college classes. They can study areas such as surgery or animal teeth.

Famous Veterinarians

Claude Bourgelat started the first vet college. He opened it in 1761 in Lyon, France. Students there worked to stop animal sickness in Europe. By 1852, the first American vet school opened in Philadelphia.

James Steele became a vet in 1941. Dr. Steele is famous for his work linking animal and human health.

Dr. James Steele

Fast Facts

- **What Vets Do:**
  They take care of and treat sick animals.

- **Key Clothes:**
  white lab coat, scrubs, or boots and coveralls

- **Key Tools:**
  stethoscope, x-ray, knives, scissors

- **Education Needed:**
  at least eight years of college

- **Key Function:**
  caring for animals

- **Famous Veterinarians:**
  Claude Bourgelat and Dr. James Steele

Glossary

aquarium (uh-KWAYR-ee-uhm)—a place that exhibits many types of live fish and other ocean life

exercise (EK-suhr-syz)—physical activity done in order to stay healthy

medicine (MED-uh-suhn)—a drug or other substance used to treat a sickness

scrubs (SKRUBZ)—loose, lightweight clothes worn by workers in clinics, hospitals, and some veterinarian offices

shelter (SHEL-tur)—a place that takes care of lost or stray animals

stethoscope (STETH-uh-skope)—a tool used to listen to the heart and lungs

surgery (SUR-jer-ee)—an operation that involves cutting into the body to remove or fix a part of the body

X-ray (EKS-ray)—a picture taken of the inside of the body that can show if something is wrong

Read More

Ardely, Anthony. *I Can Be a Veterinarian*. New York, NY: Gareth Stevens Publishing, 2019.

Bedell, J. M. *So, You Want to Work with Animals?: Discover Fantastic Ways to Work with Animals, from Veterinary Science to Aquatic Biology*. New York, NY: Aladdin, 2017.

Meister, Cari. *Veterinarians*. Minneapolis, MN: 9 Bull Frog Books, 2015.

Internet Sites

6 Books for Future Veterinarians
https://www.barnesandnoble.com/blog/kids/books-aspiring-veterinarians/

Games: Become a Vet
https://www.vetsetgo.com/games

Veterinarian Games and Activities
https://www.educatall.com/page/449/Veterinarians.html

Index